George Washington Julian

Radicalism and conservation

The truth of history vindicated

George Washington Julian

Radicalism and conservation
The truth of history vindicated

ISBN/EAN: 9783337893927

Printed in Europe, USA, Canada, Australia, Japan

Cover: Foto ©ninafisch / pixelio.de

More available books at **www.hansebooks.com**

SPEECH

OF

HON. GEO. W. JULIAN, OF INDIANA,

IN THE HOUSE OF REPRESENTATIVES,

FEBRUARY 7, 1865.

The House being in the Committee of the Whole on the State of the Union, and having under consideration the President's message—

Mr. JULIAN said:

Mr. CHAIRMAN: Perhaps no task could be more instructive or profitable, in these culminating days of the rebellion, than a review of the shifting phases of thought and policy which have guided the Administration in its endeavors to crush it. Such a retrospect will help us to vindicate the real truth of history, both as to measures and men. It will bring out, in the strongest colors, the contrast between radicalism and conservatism, as rival political forces, each maintaining a varying control over the conduct of the war. It will, at the same time, point out and emphasize those pregnant lessons of the struggle which may best supply the Government with counsel in its further prosecution. The faithful performance of this task demands plainness of speech; and I shall not shrink from my accustomed use of it, in the interests of truth and freedom.

At the beginning of this war, Mr. Chairman, neither of the parties to it comprehended its character and magnitude. Its actual history has been an immeasurable surprise to both, and to the whole civilized world. The rebels evidently expected to make short work of it. Judging us by our habitual and long-continued submission to Southern domination, and confiding in the multiplied assurances of sympathy and help which they had received from their faithful allies in the North, they regarded the work of dismemberment as neither difficult nor expensive. They did not dream of the grand results which have proceeded from their mad enterprise. Nor does their delusion seem to have been at all strange or unnatural. Certainly, it was not more remarkable than the infatuation of the Administration, and its conservative friends. The Government understood

the conflict as little, and misunderstood it as absolutely, as its foes. This, sir, is one of the lessons of the war which I think it worth while to have remembered. This revolt, it was believed, was simply a new and enlarged edition of Southern bluster. The Government did not realize the inexorable necessity of actual war, because it lacked the moral vision to perceive the real nature of the contest. To every suggestion of so dire an event it turned an averted face and a deaf ear. It hoped to restore order by making a show of war, without actually calling into play the terrible enginery of war. It trusted in the form, without the power of war, just as some people have trusted in the form, without the power of godliness. It will be remembered that just before the battle of Ball's Bluff General McClellan ordered Colonel Stone to "make a slight demonstration against the rebels," which might "have the effect to drive them from Leesburg." The Government seems to have pursued a like policy in dealing with the rebellion itself. "A slight demonstration," it was believed, would "have the effect" to arrest the rebels in their madness, and re-establish order and peace in about "sixty days," without allowing them to be seriously hurt, and without unchaining the tiger of war at all. The philosophy of General Patterson, who kindly advised that the war on our part should be "conducted on peace principles," was by no means out of fashion with our rulers, and the conservative leaders of opinion generally. Even the Commander-in-Chief of our Army and Navy scouted the idea of putting down the rebellion by military power. He thought the country was to be saved by giving up the principles it had fairly won by the ballot in the year 1860, and to the maintenance of which the new Administration was solemnly pledged. He believed in "conciliation," in "compromise"— the meanest word in the whole vocabulary of our politics, except, perhaps, the word "conservative"—and had far less faith in the help of bullets and bayonets in managing the rebels than in the power of our brotherly love to melt their susceptible hearts, and woo them back, gently and lovingly, to a sense of their madness and their crime. Our distinguished Secretary of State declared that "none but a despotic or imperial Government would seek to subjugate thoroughly disaffected sovereignties." The policy of coercing the revolted States was disavowed by the President himself in his message to Congress of July, 1861.

Nor did the legislative department of the Government, at that time, disagree with the executive. On the 22d day of July of the same year—and I say it with sorrow and shame—on the very morning following the first battle of Bull Run, the House of Representatives, speaking in the form of solemn legislative resolves, as did the Senate two days later, declared that it was not the purpose of the Government to "subjugate" the villains who began this work of organized and inexcusable rapine and murder. Indeed, it was not then the fashion to call them villains. In the very polite and gingerly phrase of the times they were styled "our misguided fellow-citizens," and "our erring Southern brethren," while the rebel States themselves were lovingly referred to as "our wayward sisters." The truth is, that for about a year and a half of this war the policy of tenderness to the rebels so swayed the Administration that it seemed far less intent upon crushing the rebellion by arms, than upon contriving "how *not* to do it." General McClellan, who so long palsied the energies and balked the purpose of the nation, would not allow an unkind word to be uttered in his presence against the rebel leaders. If an officer or soldier was heard to speak disrespectfully of the great confederate chief, he was summarily reprimanded, while the unrivaled reprobate and grandest of national cut-throats was pronounced a high-souled gentleman and man of honor! Not the spirit of war, but the spirit of peace, seemed to dictate our principles of action and measures of policy toward the men who had resolved, at whatever hazard or sacrifice, to break up the Government by force. This policy, sir, had it been continued, would have proved the certain triumph of the rebel cause. With grand armies in the field, and all the costly machinery of war in our hands, our opportunities were sinned away by inactivity and delay, while the rebels gathered strength from our indecision and weakness. A major general in our army, and as brave and patriotic a man as lives, said to me in the early stages of the war that the grand obstacle to our success was the lack of resentment on our part toward traitors. He said we did not adequately hate them; and he urged me, if in any degree in my power, to breathe into the hearts of the people in the loyal States a spirit of righteous indignation and wrath toward the rebels commensurate with the unmatched enormity of their deeds.

This spirit, Mr. Chairman, was a military necessity. The absence of it furnishes the best explanation of our failure during the period referred to, while its acceptance by the Government inaugurated the new policy which has ever since been giving us victories.

That this sickly policy of an inoffensive war has naturally prolonged the struggle, and greatly augmented its cost in blood and treasure, no one can doubt. That it belongs, with its entire legacy of frightful results, exclusively to the conservative element in our politics, which at first ruled the Government, is equally certain. The radical men saw at first, as clearly as they see to-day, the character and spirit of this rebel revolt. The massacre at Fort Pillow, the starvation of our soldiers at Richmond, and the whole black catalogue of rebel atrocities, have only been so many verified predictions of the men who had studied the institution of slavery, and who regarded the rebellion as the natural fruit and culmination of its Christless career. And hence it was that in the very beginning of the war, radical men were in favor of its vigorous prosecution. They knew the foe with whom we had to wrestle. In language employed on this floor more than three years ago, they knew that "sooner than fail in their purpose the rebels would light up heaven itself with the red glare of the pit, and convert the earth into a carnival of devils." They knew that "every weapon in the armory of war must be grasped, and every arrow in our quiver sped toward the heart of a rebel." They knew that "all tenderness to such a foe is treason to our cause, murder to our people, faithlessness to the grandest and holiest trust ever committed to a free people." They knew that "the war should be made just as terrific to the rebels as possible, consistently with the laws of war, not as a work of vengeance, but of mercy, and the surest means of our triumph." They knew that in struggling with such a foe we were shut up to one grand and inevitable necessity and duty, and that was entire and absolute *subjugation*. All this was avowed and insisted upon by the earnest men who understood the nature of the conflict, and as persistently disavowed and repudiated by the Government and its conservative advisers.

But a time came when its lessons had to be unlearned. In the school of trial it was forced to admit that war does not mean peace, but exactly the opposite of peace. Slowly, and step by step, it yielded up its theories and brought itself face to face with the stern facts of the crisis. The Government no longer gets frightened at the word subjugate, because of its literal etymology, but is manfully and successfully endeavoring to place the yoke of the Constitution upon the unbaptised necks of the scoundrels who have thrown it off. The war is now recognized as a struggle of numbers, of desperate physical violence, to be fought out to the bitter end, without stopping to count its cost in money or in blood. Both the people and our armies, under this new dispensation, have been learning how to hate rebels as Christian patriots ought to have done from the beginning. They have been learning how to hate rebel sympathizers also, and to brand them as even meaner than rebels outright. They regard the open-throated traitor, who stakes his life, his property, his all, upon the success of his conspiracy against the Constitution and the rights of man, as a more tolerable character than the skulking miscreant who in his heart wishes the rebellion God-speed, while masquerading in the hypocritical disguise of loyalty. Had the Government been animated by a like spirit at the beginning of the outbreak, practically accepting the truth that there can be no middle ground between treason and loyalty, rebel sympathizers would have given the country far less trouble than they have done. A little wholesome severity, summarily administered, would have been a most sovereign panacea. On this point the people were in advance of the Administration, and they are to-day. Their earnestness has not yet found a complete and authoritative expression in the action of the Government. A system of retaliation, which would have been a measure of real mercy, has not yet been adopted. Our cause is not wholly rescued from the control of conservative politicians and generals. Much remains to be done; but far more, certainly, has already been accomplished. The times of brotherly love towards rebels in arms have gone by forever. Such men as McClellan, Buell, and Fitz John Porter, are generally out of the way, and men who believe in *fighting* rebels are in active command. This revolution in the war policy of the Government, as already observed, was absolutely necessary to the salvation of our cause; and the country will not soon forget those earnest men who at first comprehended the crisis and the duty, and persistently urged a vigorous policy, suited to remorseless and revolutionary violence, till the Government felt constrained to embrace it.

But a vigorous prosecution of the war, Mr. Chairman, was not enough. While this struggle is one of numbers and of violence, it is likewise, and still more emphatically, a war of ideas; a conflict between two forms of civilization, each wresting for the mastery of the country. No one now pretends to dispute this, nor is it easy to understand how any one could ever have failed to perceive it. But the Government, in the beginning, did not believe it. It tried, with all its might, not to believe it, and to persuade the world to disbelieve it. It insisted that the real cause of the war did not cause it at all. The rebellion was the work of chance; a stupendous accident, leaping into life full-grown, without father or mother, without any discoverable genesis. It was a huge, black, portentous, national riot, which must be suppressed, but nobody was to be allowed to say one word about the causes which produced it, or the issues involved in the struggle. Silence was to be our supreme wisdom. Hence it was that the Government, speaking through its high functionaries, declared that the slavery question was not involved in the quarrel, and that every slave in bondage would remain in exactly the same condition after the war as before. Hence it was that, when a celebrated proclamation was issued, giving freedom to slaves of rebels in Missouri, it was revoked by the Government in order to please the State of Kentucky, and placate the power that began the war. Hence, under General Halleck's "Order No. 3," which remained in force more than a year, the swarms of contrabands who came thronging to our lines, tendering us the use of their muscles and the secrets of the rebel prison-house, were driven away by our commanders. Hence it was that our soldiers were compelled to serve as slave-hounds in chasing down fugitives and sending them back to rebel masters, and that General McClellan, who always loved slavery more than he loved his country, and who declared he would put down slave insurrections "with an iron hand," was continued as commander-in-chief of our armies long months after the country desired to spew him out. Hence, likewise, so many thousands of our soldiers were compelled to dig and ditch in the swamps of the Chickahominy till the cold sweat of death gathered on the handle of the spade, while swarms of stalwart negroes, able to relieve them and eager to do so, were denied the privilege, lest it should offend the nostrils of democratic gentility, and give aid and comfort to the Abolitionists. Hence it was that the President, instead of striking at slavery as a military necessity, and while rebuking that policy in his dealings with Hunter and Fremont, was at the same time so earnestly espousing chimerical projects for the colonization of negroes, coupled with the policy of gradual and compensated emancipation, which should take place some time before the year 1900, if the slaveholders should be willing. Hence it was that very soon after the Administration had been installed in power it began to lose sight of the principles on which it had triumphed in 1860, allowing four-fifths of the offices of the army and navy to be held by men of known hostility to those principles, while the various departments of the Government in this city were largely filled by rebel sympathizers. Hence it was that for nearly two years of this war the Government, while smiting the rebels with one hand, was with the other guarding the slave property and protecting the constitutional rights of the men who had renounced the Constitution, and ceased to have any rights under it save the right to its penalty against traitors. Hence it was that during the greater part of this time the Administration stood upon the platform and urged the policy of "the Constitution as it is and the Union as it was," which the nation so overwhelmingly repudiated in the late presidential contest. Hence it was finally, that the songs of Whittier could not be sung in our armies; that slavery was everywhere dealt with by the Government as the dear child of its love; and that our rulers seemed, with matchless impiety, to hope for the favor of God without laying hold of the *conscience* of our quarrel, and by coolly kicking it out of doors! Sir, I believe it safe to say that this madness cost the nation the precious sacrifice of fifty thousand soldiers, who have gone up to the throne of God as witnesses against the horrid infatuation that so long shaped the policy of the Government in resisting this slaveholders' rebellion.

But here, again, Mr. Chairman, the Government had to unlearn its first lessons. Its purpose to crush the rebellion and spare slavery was found to be utterly suicidal to our cause. It was a purpose to accomplish a moral impossibility, and was therefore prosecuted, if not conceived, in the interest of the rebels. It was an attempt to marry treason and loyalty; for the rebellion *is* slavery, armed with the powers of war, organized for wholesale schemes of aggression, and animated by the overflowing fullness of its infernal genius. The strength of our cause lies in its righteousness, and therefore no bargain with the devil could possibly give it aid. Through great suffering and sacrifice, individual and national, our rulers learned that there is but "one strong thing here below, the just thing, the true thing," and that God would not allow these severed States to be reunited without the abandonment, forever, of our great national sin. This was a difficult lesson, but as it was gradually mastered the Government "changed its base." It became disenchanted. Congress took the lead in ushering in the new dispensation. A new Article of War was enacted, forbidding our armies from returning fugitive slaves. Slavery was abolished in the District of Columbia, and prohibited in our national Territories, where it had been planted by the dogma of popular sovereignty and the Dred Scott decision. Our Federal judiciary was so reorganized as to make sure this anti-slavery legislation of Congress. The confiscation of slaves was provided for, and freedom offered to all who would come over and help us, either as laborers or soldiers, thus annulling the famous and *infamous* order of General Halleck, already referred to. The fugitive slave law was at first made void as to the slaves of rebels, and finally repealed altogether, with the old law of 1793. The coastwise slave trade, a frightful system of home piracy, carried on by authority of Congress since the year 1807, was totally abolished. The right of testimony in our Federal courts, and to sue and be sued, was conferred upon negroes. Their employment as soldiers was at last systematically provided for, and their pay at length made the same as that of white soldiers. The independence of Hayti and Liberia was recognized, and new measures taken to put an end to the African slave trade. In thus wiping out our code of national slave laws, acknowledging the manhood of the negro, and recognizing slavery as the enemy of our peace, Congress emphatically rebuked the policy which had sought to ignore

it, and to shield it from the destructive hand of the war instigated by itself; while it opened the way for further and inevitable measures of justice, looking to his complete emancipation from the dominion of Anglo-Saxon prejudice, the repeal of all special legislation intended for his injury, and his absolute restoration to equal rights with the white man as a citizen as well as a soldier.

Meanwhile, the President had been giving the subject his sober second thought, and reconsidering his position at the beginning of the conflict. Instead of affirming, as at first, that the question of slavery was not involved in the struggle, he gradually perceived and finally admitted that it was at once the cause of the war and the obstacle to peace. Instead of resolving to save the Union *with* slavery, he finally resolved to save the Union without it, and by its destruction. Instead of entertaining the country with projects of gradual and distant emancipation, conditioned upon compensation to the master and the colonization of the freedmen, he himself finally launched the policy of immediate and unconditional liberation. Instead of recoiling from "radical and extreme measures," and "a remorseless revolutionary conflict," he at last marched up to the full height of the national emergency, and proclaimed "to all whom it may concern," that slavery must perish. Instead of a constitutional amendment for the purpose of eternizing the institution in the Republic, indorsed by him in his inaugural message, he became the zealous advocate of a constitutional amendment abolishing it forever. Instead of committing the fortunes of the war to pro-slavery commanders, whose hearts were not in the work, he learned how to dispense with their services, and find the proper substitutes. These forward movements were not ventured upon hastily, but after much hesitation and apparent reluctance. Not suddenly, but following great deliberation and many misgivings, he issued his proclamation of freedom. Months afterward he doubted its wisdom; but it was a grand step forward, which at once severed his relations with his old conservative friends, and linked his fortunes thenceforward to those of the men of ideas and of progress. Going hand in hand with Congress in the great advance measures referred to, or acquiescing in their adoption, the whole policy of the Administration has been revolutionized. Abolitionism and loyalty are now accepted as convertible terms, and so are treason and slavery. Our covenant with death is annulled. Our national partnership with Satan has been dissolved; and just in proportion as this has been done, and an alliance sought with divine Providence, has the cause of our country prospered. In a word, Radicalism has saved our nation from the political damnation and ruin to which conservatism would certainly have consigned it; while the mistakes and failures of the Administration stand confessed in its new policy, which alone can vindicate its wisdom, command the respect and gratitude of the people, and save it from humiliation and disgrace.

Mr. Chairman, these lessons of the past suggest the true moral of this great conflict, and make the way of the future plain. They demand a vigorous prosecution of the war by all the powers of war, and that the last vestige of slavery shall be scourged out of life. Let the Administration falter on either of these points and the people will disown its policy. They have not chosen the President for another term through any secondary or merely personal considerations. In the presence of so grand an issue, men were nothing. They had no faith in General McClellan and the party leaders at his heels. They had little faith in the early policy of Mr. Lincoln, when Democratic ideas ruled his Administration, and the power of slavery held him in its grasp. Had his appeal to the people been made two years earlier, he would have been as overwhelmingly repudiated as he has been gloriously indorsed. The people sustain him now, because of their assured faith that he will not hesitate to execute their will. In voting for him for a second term, they voted for liberating and arming the slaves of the South to crush out a slaveholders' rebellion. They voted that the Republic shall live, and that whatever is necessary to save its life shall be done. They voted that slavery shall be eternally doomed, and future rebellions thus made impossible. They voted, not that Abraham Lincoln can save the country, but that *they* can save it, with him as their servant. That is what was decided in the late elections. I have participated, somewhat actively, in seven presidential contests, and I remember none in which the element of personal enthusiasm had a smaller share than that of last November. One grand and overmastering resolve filled the hearts and swayed the purposes of the masses everywhere, and that was the rescue of the country through the defeat of the Chicago platform and conspirators. In the execution of that resolve they lost sight of everything else; but should the President now place himself in the people's way, by reviving the old policy of tenderness to the rebels and their beloved institution, the loyal men of the country will abandon his policy as decidedly as they have supported it generously. They have not approved the mistakes either of the legislative or executive department of the Government. they expect that Congress will pass a bill for the confiscation of the fee of rebel landholders, and they expect the President will approve it. They expect that Congress will provide for the reconstruction of the rebel States by systematic legislation, which shall guarantee republican governments to each of those States, and the complete enfranchisement of the negro; and they will not approve, as they have not approved, of any executive interference with the people's will as deliberately expressed by Congress. They expect that Congress will provide for parceling out the forfeited and confiscated lands of rebels in small homesteads among the soldiers and

seamen of the war, as a fit reward for their valor, and a security against the ruinous monopoly of the soil in the South; and they will be disappointed should this great measure fail through the default either of Congress or the Executive. They demand a system of just retaliation against the rebels for outrages committed upon our prisoners; that a policy of increasing earnestness and vigor shall prevail till the war shall be ended; and that no hope of peace shall be whispered, save on condition of an absolute and unconditional surrender to our authority; and the Government will only prolong the war by standing in the way of these demands. This is emphatically the people's war; and it will not any longer suffice to say that the people are not ready for all necessary measures of success. The people would have been ready for such measures from the beginning, if the Government had led the way. At every stage of the contest they have hailed with joy every earnest man who came forward, and every vigorous war measure that has been proposed. So long as the war was conducted under the counsels of conservatives, and in the interests of slavery, the people clamored against the Administration; but just so soon as the Government entered upon a vigorous policy, and proclaimed war against slavery, the people began to shout for the Union and liberty. In the fall of 1862, before the Administration was divorced from its early policy, the Union party was overwhelmed at the polls. But we triumphed the next year, and gloriously triumphed last year, because the Government yielded to the popular demand. The plea often urged that the people were not ready, is less a fact than a pretext. The men who loved slavery more than they loved the Union were never ready for radical measures. They are not ready to-day. On the other hand, the men who were all the while unconditionally for the Union would have sustained the Administration far more heartily in the most thorough and sweeping war measures, than they sustained its policy of delaying those measures to the last hour.

The truth is, the people have stood by the Government for the sake of the cause, whether its policy pleased them or not. Their faith and patience have been singularly unflinching throughout the entire struggle. They would not distrust the President without the strongest reasons. They were ever ready to credit him with good intentions, and to presume in favor of his superior means of knowledge. When General Fremont was recalled from Missouri, and General Butler from New Orleans, the people pocketed their deep disappointment, and quietly acquiesced. When General Buell was kept in command so long after his inefficiency had been demonstrated and his loyalty questioned, both by the country and the men under his command, the people bore it with uncommon patience and long-suffering. They displayed the same virtues in the case of General McClellan, and other rebel sympathizers, who found favor with the Administration long after the country would have sent them adrift. Sir, this feeling of unconquerable respect for our chosen rulers, this Anglo-Saxon regard for constituted authority, has been evinced by the people through all the phases of the war. Most assuredly it would not have been found wanting had the Government inaugurated a radical policy, instead of a conservative one, during the first year and a half of the struggle. The people who endured McClellan, and Buell, and Halleck, would have endured Fremont, and Hunter, and Butler. If the conservative Unionists of Kentucky were not ready for the proclamation of freedom to the slaves of Missouri rebels, there were millions of people outside of Kentucky who were not ready to have it revoked. I agree that slavery had done much to drug the conscience of the country with its insidious poison. I know that we had so long made our bed with slaveholders that kicking them out was rather an awkward business. As brethren, living under a common Government, we had long journeyed together, and our habits and traditions naturally took the form of obstacles to a just policy in dealing with them as rebels and public enemies. It was by no means easy at once to recognize them as such. All this is granted, and that in the beginning the country was not prepared for every radical measure of legislation and war now being employed by the Government. But it was the duty of the Administration to do its part in preparing the country. Clothed with solemn official authority, and intrusted by the nation with the sworn duty of serving it in such a crisis, it had no right to become the foot-ball of events. It had no right, at such a time, to make itself, a negative expression, or an unknown quantity, in the algebra which was to work out the grand problem. It had no right to take shelter beneath a debauched and sickly public sentiment, and plead it in bar of the great duty imposed upon it by the crisis. It had no right, certainly, to lag behind that sentiment, to magnify its extent and potency, and to become its virtual ally, instead of endeavoring to control it, and to indoctrinate the country with ideas suited to the emergency. The power of the Government in molding the general opinion and feeling was immense, and its responsibility must be measured accordingly. The revocation of the first anti-slavery proclamation of this war chilled the heart of every earnest loyalist in the land, and came like a trumpet-call to the pro-slavery hosts to rally and stand together. They obeyed it, and from that event dates the birth of organized copperhead democracy. The rebels of the South and their sympathizers in the North felt that they had gained an ally in the President. Had he sustained that measure, would not its moral effect have been at least as potent on the other side? Had his official name and sanction been as often given to the cause of radicalism as they were lent to that of pro-slavery conservatism would not the country have been much sooner prepared for the saving and only policy?

If he had said, early in the struggle, "to all whom it may concern," what he says now, that slavery is the nation's enemy, and therefore must be destroyed, instead of sheltering it under the Constitution and sparing it from the hand of war, how grandly could he have "organized victory" and multiplied himself among the people! Sir, our traditionary respect for slavery and slaveholders was our grand peril. It stood up as an impassable barrier in the way of any successful war for the Union. So long as it was allowed to dominate, it unnerved the arm of the Government and deadened the spirit of the people. It made the Old World our enemy, and threatened us with foreign war. The mission of the Government was not to make this feeling stronger by deferring to it, or to doom the country to a prolonged war and deplorable sacrifices as the best means of teaching the people the truth. No. The country needed a speedy exodus from the bondage of false ideas, and the Government should have pointed the way. A frank statement by it of the real issue of the war, without any disposition to cover up the truth; an unmistakable hostility to slavery as the organized curse, without which the rebellion would have been impossible; and the timely utterance in its leading State papers of a few bold and spirit-stirring words which might have been "half battles," appealing to the courage and manhood of the nation, would have gone far to educate the judgment and conscience of the people, and command their enthusiastic espousal of whatever measures would promise most speedily to end the struggle and economize its cost in property and life.

Mr. Chairman, I take no pleasure, certainly, in thus freely discussing the policy of the Government in its endeavors to meet its great responsibilities during this war. I have only referred to its mistakes as a servant of the truth, and in the name of the great cause which has been made to suffer. I believe, religiously, in the freedom of speech. From the beginning of the war I have exercised the right of frank, friendly, and fearless criticism of the conduct of our rulers, wherever I believed them to have been in the wrong. I shall continue to exercise it to the end; and if I should not, through any personal or prudential considerations, I would be unworthy of the seat I have occupied on this floor. Criticism has dictated the present policy of the Government, and is still a duty. This great battle for the rights of man, and the actors in it, must be judged. None of them can "escape history." The fame of none of them is so precious as the truth, and as public justice, which cares for the dead as well as the living, for the common soldiers slain by thousands, as well as for the general and the statesman. The President, his advisers, his commanding generals, and the civilians whose shaping hands have had so much to do with the conduct of the war, must all of them be weighed in the balance by the people and the generations to come. "The great soul of the world is just," and sooner or later all disguises will be thrown off, and every historical character will stand forth as he is, in the light of his deeds and deserts. The men who have been intrusted with the concerns of the nation in this momentous crisis will not be judged harshly. Much will be forgiven or excused on the score of the surpassing magnitude and difficulty of their work. Justice will be done; but that justice may brand as a crime, the blunders proceeding from a feeble, timid, ambidextrous policy, resulting in great sacrifices of life and treasure, and periling the priceless interests at stake. I would award all due honor to this Administration, and to the statesmen and generals who have been faithful to their high trusts; but I would award an equal honor to the rank and file of the people, who have inspired its present policy, and to the rank and file of our soldiers, who have saved the country in spite of the mistakes of the Government, the strifes of our politicians, and the rivalries of our generals. These are the real heroes of the war. Untitled, practically unrewarded, facing every form of privation and danger, and animated by the purest patriotism, the common soldier is not only the true hero of the war, but the real saviour of his country.

But a higher honor, if not a more enduring fame, will be the heritage of the anti-slavery pioneers and prophets of our land; for

" Peace hath higher tests of manhood
 Than battle ever knew."

Without their heroic labors and sacrifices the Republic, " heir of all the ages," would have been the mightiest slave empire of the world. In an age of practical atheism and mammon-worship, when the Church and the State joined hands with Slavery as the new trinity of the nation's faith, they really believed in God, in justice, in the resistless might of the truth. They believed that liberty is the birthright of all men, and their grand mission was the practical vindication of this truth. They believed, with their whole hearts, in the Declaration of Independence. They accepted its teachings as coincident with the gospel of Christ, and supported by reason and justice. It was their ceaseless " battle-cry of freedom," and they chanted it as " the fresh, the matin song of the universe," to the enslaved of all races and lands. They were branded as fanatics and infidels, and encountered everywhere the hootings of the multitude and the scorn of politicians and priests; but I know of no class of men who were ever more far-sighted, whose convictions rested on so broad a basis of Christian morals and logic, and whose religious trust was so strong and so steadfast. For them there was no " eclipse of faith." Just as the nation began to lapse from the grand ideas of our revolutionary era, they began to " cry aloud and spare not," and they never ceased or slackened their labors. Placing their ears to the ground in the infancy and weakness of their movement, they caught the rumbling thunders of civil war in the distance, warned the country of its danger, and preached repent-

ance as the chosen and only means of escape. They were compelled to face mobs, violence, persecution, and death, and were always misunderstood or misrepresented; but they never faltered. Reputation, honors, property, worldly ease, were all freely laid upon the altar of duty, in their resolve to vindicate the rights of man and the freedom of speech. To follow these apostles and martyrs was to forsake all the prizes of life which worldly prudence or ambition could value or covet. It was to take up the heaviest cross yet fashioned by this century as the test of Christian character and heroism; and those who bore it were far braver spirits than the men who fight our battles on land and sea.

Mr. Chairman, the failure of men thus devoted to a great and holy cause was morally impossible. They could not fail. Through their courage, constancy, and faith, they gradually received the co-operation or sympathy of the better type of men of all parties and creeds. They seriously disturbed, or broke in pieces, the great political and ecclesiastical organizations of the land: and even before this war their ideas were rapidly taking captive the popular heart. When it came, they saw, as by intuition, the character of the struggle, as the final phase of slaveholding madness and crime, and insisted upon the early adoption of that radical policy which the Government at last was compelled to accept. I believe it safe to say that the moral appeals and persistent criticism of these men, and of the far greater numbers who borrowed or sympathized with their views, saved our cause from the complete control of conservatism, and thus saved the country itself from destruction. Going at once to the heart of our great conflict, they pointed out the only remedy, and felt compelled to reprobate the failure of the Government to adopt it. They judged its policy in war, as they had done in peace, in the light of its fidelity or infidelity to human rights. By this test they tried every man and party, and they need ask for no other rule of judgment for themselves. The Administration, and the chief actors in this drama of war, of whatever political school, must be weighed in the same great balance. Not even the founders of the Republic will be spared from the trial. In their compromise with slavery in the beginning, which is now seen to have been the germ of this horrid conflict, they " swerved from the right." Posterity must so pronounce; and the record which dims the luster of their great names will be read in the flames of this war as a warning against all future compacts with evil. Justice to public men is as certain as that truth is omnipotent. It may be delayed for a season; it may be hidden from the vision of men of little faith; but its final triumph is sure. To the world's true heroes and confessors history ever sends its word of cheer:

" The good can well afford to wait;
 Give ermined knaves their hour of crime;
 Ye have the future, grand and great,
 The safe appeal of truth to time."

.